THE LONG HABIT OF LIVING

THE LONG HABIT OF LIVING

M. R. Peacocke

HAPPENSTANCE PRESS

© M. R. Peacocke, 2021

ISBN: 978-1-910131-68-8

Acknowledgements:

Thanks to editors of the following in which some of these poems, or earlier versions, first appeared or are forthcoming: *Artemis*, *The Dark Horse*, *The Friday Poem* (online), *The Lyrical Aye (*online), *The North*.

Seven of the poems were previously included in a pamphlet: *Honeycomb* (see below).

Publications by M. R. Peacocke:

- *Broken Ground* (prose memoir), Shoestring Press, 2018
- *Honeycomb* (pamphlet), Happen*Stance* Press, 2018
- *Finding the Planes,* Shoestring Press, 2015
- *Caliban Dancing*, Shoestring Press, 2013
- *In Praise of Aunts,* Peterloo Poets, 2011
- *Speaking of the Dead*, Peterloo Poets, 2003
- *Selves,* Peterloo Poets, 1995
- *Marginal Land,* Peterloo Poets, 1988

First published in 2021 by Happen*Stance* Press
21 Hatton Green, Glenrothes KY7 4SD
https://happenstancepress.com

All rights reserved

The right of M. R. Peacocke to be identified as author of this work has been asserted in accordance with the Copyright, Designs & Patent Act, 1988

Printed and bound by Imprint Digital, Exeter
https://digital.imprint.co.uk

Contents

Book / 9

Syllabary / 10

Practice / 11

Strike / 12

Rockabye / 13

Put / 14

Beetle / 15

Flies / 16

Gig Economy / 17

Moth / 18

Beast / 19

Exercise / 20

Leaving / 21

Rembrandt's Pen / 22

Candling Eggs / 23

Sweet Thames / 24

Air Letters / 25

White / 26

Winter Festival / 27

Dust / 28

Some Saints / 29

The Clever Girls / 30

The Watcher at the Window / 31

The Maid's Tale / 32

From Recent Records / 33

From Captain Cook's Journal, July 1770 / 34

The Path through the Wood / 36

A Walk with William Blake / 37

The Palace at Six O'Clock / 38

The Minotaur Problem / 39

Jonah's Tale / 40

The Sisters / 42

Exposures / 43

Evacuees' Outing, 1940 / 44

The Wooden House / 46

What Remains / 47

Skin Narratives / 48

These Hands / 49

Clinic / 50

False Step / 51

Counting / 52

How the Story Goes / 53

Five / 54

Reflex / 55

The One Chosen / 56

The Gardener / 57

What the Bird Said / 58

Mote / 59

Theend / 60

Dunnerholm / 61

The Pebble / 62

About the author / 64

'The long habit of living indisposeth us for dying'

—Sir Thomas Browne, *Urne-Buriall*, 1656

BOOK

The Book of the unknown foetus.
The Book of cats in bags, pigs in pokes,
Moses in baskets with all the eggs.
The Book of errors, terrors, accidents (happy),
accidents (unhappy, Vol. II).

The Book of rambling worms and moths,
half a page, half a page onward, coding
and ciphering in plainsong,
perishing under the rose.
The Book of random inclinations,

of keys, doors, entrances, exits
with bears, sniggering under sheets,
loves on the brink of hatreds, holy
alliances, barefoot dances,
losses, peregrine snatches.

The Book of direct and indirect speech,
The Book of lies hidden in plain sight
which omits what most matters, riddling
Lazarus gospel. Thumb through it if you must,
it's written and can't be amended, this book.

SYLLABARY

Literacy was expected
of that child. Her formal father
snipped small picture cards: pen, cup, bed.
She sat (mat, pat) on an upright chair
until she had mastered those glyphs. Then
she could be pleased and jump down.

Away in the garden, the wall
never bothered with warnings (tall, fall),
nor the trees with regular form. The wind
sang and shouted for its own delight,
the whole green world its playground.
Clouds scribbled and smudged out.

Later, a phone rhymed and rhymed.
There lay somebody dying, defying
inarticulacy. A rabble of sound
marched for him at random,
syllables in limbo.
His eyes could have burned snow.

PRACTICE

She haunts me with a bridled patience,
and when she comes, as now she's come,
my heart keeps stumbling, can't perform
as it agrees it should; but *Nonsense,
Darling*, she cries—she is crying—clinches
of irritation in her throat, and shame
obstructing mine—*It simply needs more time,
more time and work, until it's effortless!*
But in her smile and in her spine
there's effort, as in her turn of phrase.
Her ash is in my hair. My god,
can't she accept how it is to be dead?
While I still blame her, she can know no peace,
her yearning and critical heart being mine.

STRIKE

The axe bit. Out tumbled the grocery yellows.
The old stump flaked like a haddie, crumbled like cheese.

So many small peculiar creatures legging it
or on their backs in a slow sprawl, or brought up short
with half a body, as though they'd been keeping shop
or shopping, when an earthquake struck or a bomb fell.

Sunface wipes his forehead, leaning over the haft,
and gazes from the raw blue at their distraction.

ROCKABYE

Wind rakes the highwire lodges.
A bough breaks, and down go all
the babies, the quilled gapers
smashed in a porridge of leaves,
while the rooks cry endlessly
at the huddle of absence,
the outrage of vanished mouths.

Didn't you hear? The old rhymes
(they don't lie) predicted it.
Did you think it was a dream?
Houses unroofed, walls tumbled,
windows burst, the black, distraught
figures of women scouring
among ruins. How they cried.

PUT

At last my door, and putting everything down
to fumble for the key before life to come

and becoming aware of Put: these bags, weight
of potatoes, a couple of jars, all the stuff

settling into a sideways loll, and there it is,
put: burdened but neutral, awaiting guidance,

and I'm tasting the powerlessness of the object
(though there was, once, a fear that the dead might rise)

when oh, there goes the milkman's horse, my childhood's
loved horse-mountain, moving without command but clop

by clop and stopping gate by gate, the dead stoop
of gravity in the lift and plant of his vast

and simple hooves. No decision, but inherent
in each put, the atlastness of arriving.

BEETLE

This beetle, wedging and trudging
between leaves and stems, puzzles
through a universe of accidents.
Comes upon an obstacle—
the block of my hand lying inert
in the summer grass. What is this
to his beetle sense? An Is,
part of the Among, or alien, textured
strangely in warmth and smell?

The apparatus of his head
undertakes its slow enquiries.
The object disappears. Beetle
continues his leisurely progress
unperturbed, leg by leg, until
he's faulted, tipped sidelong
on a little stone. Sunlight
reforges his blue-black shape
as a shield of absolute gleam.

FLIES

There's a rusted yellow rose tapping at the pane.
In here a bluebottle keeps veering and droning,
wanting the air to open.

I'm old, I'm like Roman glass,
no more use, carefully kept, fragile and cloudy.
Everything about me is a long time ago.

There was a kitchen where I used to play. I watched
houseflies riding an invisible carousel.
They were happy as they were,

sipping the smells. Let me out
to the ragged world, safe from sweepers and sprayers
who come in early for those of us on our backs.

GIG ECONOMY

Weeds on walls, hardy and frugal, wedded
in gambling weather to the thicks and thins
of mortar crumb, the cant and slew of stone,
bid for a place in the fickle sun.

Wallflowers' tawny flourish,
bravado of poppies caught in the nick
of light, toadflax, saxifrage set out
their stalls in the dry nomansland
of crevices and gritty cols

offering honeyed snacks to tongues
of Painted Ladies, Tortoiseshells,
King Billies, Cabbage Whites,
louche, spotted Burnet Moths
and common plundering flies.

MOTH

Somebody must have taken the snap
from an upstairs window. Monochrome,
deckle-edged. There's a woman
down on a tidy lawn, pale, dumpy,
hunched on a garden chair. She looks
like a doll some child has dropped,
running away to cuddle
one she loves better. Who pinned her
into this brown album like a moth?

BEAST

Spine hunches dry and rough
against mechanisms of the day.
Blood sulks. The heart's a nail.

Ears clench down, blunted with human noise.
Where's the pin of light
that would flare from the back of an eye?

Hope stinks, a yellow bone
in a corner by the water trough
where the stale hours drip through.

Rouse, body, enough at least to bite,
to deny or defy
an opening hatch, a keeper's care.

EXERCISE

I have tried Pushups off the wall
and *You will need a chair for this
looking straight ahead raise your leg
sideways—hold—and lower slowly
and now breathe—arms up! arms down!* Arms
straight through the window-pane. La chair
est triste et j'ai lu tous les livres
and I've had—how I've had—TV.

So this evening I managed Out
and I must thank the two young blokes
chattering up behind who shot
past either side of me, shoulders
almost touching, when the whole road
was empty: and that has made all
the difference. What happened? I yelled.
I yelled so hard they staggered,
mumbled *Sorry Ma'am* and scarpered

while sound that streamed from the bottom
of my cracked lungs astonished me.
Fatheads! Nincompoops!
                          The low sun
still shining. Nobody about
except me, brandishing my stick,
exhilarated, like the late
Sir Adrian Boult at the Proms.

Somebody tell the Ministry:
Yelling is the best exercise.

LEAVING

I saw her last in the mirror as I drove away,
a figure in the lane with hands lifted awkwardly
as though she'd dropped a cup, or was about to drop it.

I didn't much want to be off to my distant life.
I didn't want her to watch me go, although I think
she wasn't watching but seeing. I wished she'd go in.

There's not much colour, only a glimpse of the fuchsia
at the garden wall, a crimson smudge. She's not moving,
just standing there getting smaller. I can't see her face.

At the far end of the graveyard where nobody goes
I found a little statue once, arms crossed at the breast,
discarded, yet content to be there, smiling.
I keep on finding it. Over and over again.

REMBRANDT'S PEN

—After Rembrandt's sketch of his wife Saskia on her deathbed

A woman in a bed, exhausted.
A body. Any burdened body
sagging and propped in pillows.

Her breath in the closed room hangs and haunts.
Forgotten lavender of stored cloth.
The scent of loss. Thin acid.

She has buried a son, their first-born,
a daughter, and a second daughter.
Still, there's Titus. Perhaps, Titus.

Love cannot save her now, nor any
delicate broth. A hand, labouring
to preserve her line by line

moves, moves. The mouse-scratch of a fine pen
records her two hands fallen, mapping
their heaviness as it grows,

translating into a little mark
one closed eye, with the brow above it
fixed at the angle of pain.

Blanched mound of a body, simplified
in dimension, resembling silence.
Saskia, are you there? Saskia?

CANDLING EGGS

She's plumbed into immobility, the little hen,
unable to stir. You push your fingers
into the blind heat, feel for one, lift it. Pierce the shell
with your needle of light. There's the foetus
jigging in a web of scarlet, so mark its brown cot
with a pencilled cross and slip it back. Probe
for the next in the furnace she's made naked for them.
She turns her head, opens her beak, can't say
anything. All her force has sunk into her belly.
A single egg is cradling a bloodspeck,
dull, sheeted in cloudy albumen. Put it aside.

I've counted her chickens. Twelve, has she?
There's a tender brutality about life
that's not to be questioned. Soon she'll wake
to their waking, sing to them, comfort, cajole.
Some will prosper and some won't. May those
who know how to be get on with it.

SWEET THAMES

The odour of August grass and tobacco.
Pipe tobacco. The particular texture
of trousers, scratchy and narrow, with cuffs. Hair
a similar rough tweed. Sweet Thames runs softly
as my grandfather slips a hook through the flesh
of a maggot. A tin for other maggots,
Navy Cut. Tiny in the distant meadow,
portable chairs support a group of ladies
in the shade of hats. The Boer War is over.
It may be fortunate that my grandfather
has only daughters. There will be further wars,
other picnics, before I'm born; a lifetime
before I come across this snap. Grey summer.
The line is glinting. Thames continues.

AIR LETTERS

They were very dry, but time had seeped in to stain them
like spilled coffee. They rustled, and would easily burn.
A single match spurted. Flames sprang open among them,
frail blue aerogrammes shrivelling to brown.

The decayed elastic band wouldn't hold anything
together now. Writhed briefly. First the fire caressed, then
was abruptly angry, veered aside to grab stems
of nettle, twigs, leaves. Scorched at random. Shrank.

Moths of ash sat briefly on my sleeve, a ghost of script
suddenly declaring: *I...* One stubborn fragment called
from Adelaide to say *Don't forget to feed the cat,*
wasting to *Don't forget.* Finally, *Don't....*

Well, at least I've done it—posted that thin freight of news
into a little bonfire, anecdote, lies and love,
my fingers grey with it. A cremation. So, home now,
scraps of your secret life caught in my hair.

WHITE

What do I see, seeing white,
white that is never itself,
its deceptions concealing
and revealing everything?

Underwhite of a chalk cliff
sulking into stains of jade.
Clouds grizzled to losing blue.

Eel-belly thrash of water
over the weir. A white dog,
primrose against lilac snow.

The moon, once it has ripened
from mineral to bruised fruit,
blanching, returning to stone.

Accounts you give of yourself,
your eyes wide with conviction,
have that same ambivalence.
Slick as albumen, white lies.

WINTER FESTIVAL

The lights are awake in streamers and posies.
Time now to gather in the maiden aunties,
the grandmothers, settle their posture brightly
where they cannot fall, bless them with sweet sherry,
anoint their faces with well-seasoned music
and let the fires burn let the fires burn. Now stack
all the empty days into a little pile,
put a match to them, watch them flame and shrivel.

When all have eaten a slice of winter pie
it's time to fold them away fold them away
as before, follow the comfortable creases.
Happy soon, dears, happy when, happy painless.
Our rituals all are ended, the doggerel
tapped through for the year and the halting gospel
of the cold spelled out in words almost unknown
to the children, who will nod and say amen.
        Bye, Aunty. Bye, Granny. Amen.

DUST

When I am done with myself, tamp the earth well down
so that the small myriads may go unimpeded
about their work, like translators hunting the true
equivalent, or like nurses, impersonal
yet kindly, washing away my corruptions
and my weathers. Soon I shall be the mote brushed
casually from an eye, engaged for silence, made
foreign to myself element by element,
carried from soil to stem, stem to grain, grain to bread,
bread to the crumb the sparrow picks, transforms and voids.

Till now I had not understood my vocation
to be other, disparate as snow, no longer
bone, water, blood, but some multiple of dust caught
in the beam of your lamp. It's late. You turn the page,
not quite finished, the ending still speculative.
A swirl of the air. Fleck by fleck, the dust floats on.

SOME SAINTS

Here is the story of the shaggy saints
who lived on whelks and laver bread,
the stones they laid, two on one, one on two,
enough, almost, to keep the wind away.

At night they would wrap themselves in their beards
and sing raucously. The seals heard.
The choughs would bless them with guano. By day
they scraped their naked heads with oyster shells.

To find more you must lose more, so they left.
Their whitened knees and knuckles strained
towards a land of greater penitence.
The waves carried them away as trophies.

When there's a blind moon you may think of them
sailing without any lantern
in a bullhide coracle, arriving
though not quite yet, endlessly arriving.

THE CLEVER GIRLS

Hilary pay attention.
Conjugate the verb *ought*.
I ought you ought he-she-it
ought. Being infinite
ought has no infinitive

but we pretended to ought
right through to Sunday
when good Protestants keep on
oughting to the last hymn.
Only one thing can trump *ought*

and that is *must*. Hilary
must be dead. I believe
she would have died not of *ought*
but of *must*. Her father
used to sing *Oh for a rope*

to hang the Pope. His daughter
grew Roman Catholic.
I believe it's possible
to descend into hell
and leave death till afterwards.

Meanwhile, we kept well alive
folding paper arrows
full of a cargo of words,
flicking them desk to desk,
unpacking the samizdat,

witticisms, limericks,
and scribbling more, the way
I'm writing about her now,
till we could pack our books
and cross off another sun.

THE WATCHER AT THE WINDOW

One with a pouncing walk   One gliding
One engaging cautiously with flat ground
A little one running like a blackbird
the same abrupt pause   head cocked but not
to listen   only to be   There's one

pausing   weight forward weight back   fishing
in a handbag to locate a hanky
and have a snuffle   which will make progress
easier for a while   And there goes
old stiff-twin-compasses advancing

His good lady's trotting beside him
one flesh out of habit   (there was a time
when he walked with a solitary swing)
All with an aim that's just beyond sight
A bench   the Happy Isles   the corner

shop that sells everything   or simply
the turning of the planet foot by foot
so that the watching woman   who seldom
sets slipper to carpet   may still believe
that the world goes round   goes round

THE MAID'S TALE

I hadn't been in service that long. Such a morning!
I dodge out a minute, hoping no one will notice,
needing to get away from all that racket. Oh my!
You never seen so many roses in bloom at once,
thickets of them, white, crimson, stripey, alive with bees.
So I pull just one, the smell's heavenly, and nip back
in case I'm punished. I asks the lass in the pantry—
well, she stares at me and says *It's the wedding, stupid!*

Then I sees Maisie, who's mostly kind, with tears running,
 crying *He's made it through!* and there's Tom groom, he says nowt
but he's holding a big rosette. Cook's clutching her chest,
squealing *Mercy! It's turned out perfect!*—and I must say
it smelled good but I couldn't make head nor tail of it.
So in the end I goes looking for the Housekeeper
and there she is, red and bouncing with her sleeves rolled up,
quite scary she is, but I curtseys and begs to ask.

She says *Oh my lawd it's the resurrection, silly,
so will you hurry up with the breakfast, where's the eggs?*
so I'm dashing outside again—and there's this old man,
sitting on the mounting block, thin as a bone he was,
muddy all over and his eyes tight shut, but smiling.
Smiling and breathing. Then it comes to me, it's all right!
And I'm happy. Happy as a birthday, can't tell why.
I just drop my rose in his apron and fly back in.

FROM RECENT RECORDS*

No more the marl, the desert bettong
and its dwarf cousin. No more the bandicoot,
striped, from the Liverpool Plain

or the Percy Island flying fox.
Farewell, rabbit rat, and all you mice: long-eared,
blue-grey and broad-cheeked-hopping,

your excursions, investigations,
skirmishes, delicate or intemperate loves,
joys, hungers, squeaks and cries

all unrecorded. I am sad you are gone.
Nullarbor, Capricorn, your territories—
are they changed by your absence?

I had never heard of you, small lives
that seem to belong to the land of Lear. Still
the loss of you accuses.

Australian animals thought to be newly extinct

FROM CAPTAIN COOK'S JOURNAL, JULY 1770

(*A found poem with parallel accoun*t)

Mr Gore being out in the Country
shot one of the Animals afore spoke of.
It was a small one of the sort, weighing
only 28 pound clear of the entrails.

The head neck and shoulders of this Animal
was very small, the tail nearly as long
as the body, thick next the rump, tapering.
Forelegs 8 inch long and hind, 22.

Progression by hoping and jumping
7 or 8 feet upon hind legs only.
In this it makes no use of the fore: these
designed for scratching in the ground, etc.

It bears no resemblance to any
European creature I ever saw,
excepting, I thought, for the head and ears. These
something like a hare's. Fur short, a dark Mouse.

Today we dined upon the Animal
shot yesterday, and thought it excellent food.

*About the small of shadow, an odour
being perceived in our Country, we were roused
from dozing by our hearts. That strange rank air
filling our muzzles alarmed us. We marvelled*

*to see a Creature stalking leg by leg
and without any tail, unable to leap.
It stood high about our large, and the head
somewhat as birds we know, that is to say, plumed,*

*coloured and carried high: which to our startle
it removed, proceeding to rub the stump
with a paw. Each paw was greatly lengthened,
sometimes opening like a cockatoo foot,*

*or folded, perhaps for beating. One grasped
a hollow stick which breathed out hard smells of fire.
This Creature held no sort of resemblance
to any we knew since it had no pouch—though*

*it bore on its back something that might have served.
We were mightily perturbed to see it
remove some portion of its skin and then,
raising its stick towards us, to deliver*

*lightning. Our ears broke and made us leap to far.
We left our Brother kicking in his blood.*

THE PATH THROUGH THE WOOD

Through the little gate. A breath in, a breath out
measured the interim between is and is not,
the noiseless click when colour arrives at monochrome.

Blind into the wood, feeling my way, surface
by surface, gravel, grass, mud. Listening through my tread.
The ancient crepitus of the marsh became my guide,

teaching me direction in the smell of mint.
One sense became another: sigh of an odour,
taste of the darkness, fragrance of touch. My eyes found rest.

The self that walked through the wood knew more than I,
till all that had led me, left me as I stepped out—
part with relief, part with regret—into fields of stars.

A WALK WITH WILLIAM BLAKE

To have been the observer, crouching
over a pool the size that a hand
might shadow, watching a water-thread,
wavering invisible column,
rising through an aperture finer
than a needle's eye, while it juggles
mineral seed, is to understand
that the doors of perception may be
sometimes, of themselves, without effort,
cleansed. Everything appears as it is,
infinite, reconstructing itself
infinitely, unconcerned, although
there might be nobody there to see.

THE PALACE AT SIX O'CLOCK

The little Emperor in his gilded slippers
is waiting for his supper. He has rung three times.
Nobody has responded. He is vexed.
He has completed his devotions. Now
he expects his usual modest collation
before returning to Affairs of State.

There must have been some unfortunate occurrence—
soon rectified. Rectification is simple.
Disobedience, if one is clear and firm,
will vanish in an instant—*pouf!*
                                Those doves
in the courtyard: intolerably peevish.
Their foolish sound provokes irritation.

Can his men have been assaulted in the market?
The Glyph stamped on their foreheads is well recognised.
A threat would suffice and—further—one has
authority to punish. Punishment!
Murals display the Ancestral God, the Grand
Torso, sweeping away the wicked—*pouf!*

—for restoring the peace, surely the best method.
Yet how to preserve the people's love? To be loved
while maintaining order, the Emperor
must show mercy. That's only logical.
A few slow deaths should suffice. In the meantime,
where is his supper and preprandial glass?

THE MINOTAUR PROBLEM

All he could manage to do: bellow, gnash,
devour, produce dung. Must they encounter
that dead life, wade into the stench of it
to perish? They talk half in mockery,
half in disbelief, though what lies beneath
is terror, which a hero may not express.

'Hey,' says one. 'Suppose we tried drawing lots?
Short-straw blags a lantern, goes tearing in,
takes him by surprise, blasts the brightness
into those white eyes, says, *Look, you can stop;
you really can. Life's much better outside.*
And then, like: *Give me your hand—paw—whatever.*

*We're here to help. You deserve better care,
which we can get you. Warmth. Regular meals.*
Stab him later.'
                            'Hang on,' says somebody else.
'It's not a bad scheme, but the cicadas
are still at it and I'm tired. Let's just eat.
Come dawn, you bet there'll be some fool volunteer.'

JONAH'S TALE

Straight down that throat like a shucked oyster.
Hellish dark, and the boiling fluids
enough to take the rind off a pig.
Got hold of a ledge—rib, I suppose—
hoisted myself into a hideout,
same as on the ship. Roof of my mouth
thick oil, teeth full of grit. You hang on
from gasp to gasp, your lungs keep at it
willing or not. Just how many days?
No days. Night, like the one the smug priests
invoke to scare their flock to order.

Turns out I wasn't digestible.
Some kind of a riptide tore me out,
spewed me up, jetsam, good as the stuff
you'd spit onto the side of your plate.
The long and short of it: here I am,
a penitent. You work out your time.
I'd shut up about it if I could,
that gable head rough with barnacles,
every night the methuselah eye.
Like a stain you can never wash out.
Still, telling it makes me a living.

If the brave fellas ever turn up
on Tarshish quay, the ones that pitched me
overboard, out to bribe the wrong god,
tell them I'm around, the one they blamed.
Responsible for the big waves, me?
Then who knows but I've still got the knack,

so let them wait. I'm the lucky one.
That's it, brethren, and the moral is,
everybody dodgy but the fish!
You've had a good stare, so now kindly
drop a penny in my holy hat.

THE SISTERS

A good turnout, Mabel said, meaning cupboards.
Good turnout, Nora said, meaning intestines.

Oh no sugar for me, thank you, says Mabel,
upright at the neighbours' table. Nora, though,
takes two.
        Oh, says Nora, I'd love one more slice!
Mabel's a good plain cook, she was a nurse once
but she doesn't do spicy, prefers Marmite—
not in cakes, of course.
        During the war, Nora
did tea for the soldiers, Mabel says. Dunkirk ...
but thank you so much, we must be on our way,
it's the dogs, you see.
        Robert, Nora's saying,
he's Old English Sheepdog, and two Pekinese—
pity Charlie bites—and a Dandy Dinmont.

Mabel and Nora, ancient always, older
and younger (which was which?) and long departed
(who knows where?) reconciled in the love of dogs.

EXPOSURES

        –i–

What should we take? So heavy, a whole life packed up
in a canvas satchel and so long ago.
Suitcase of woven straw. Barrel of pickles.
Shofar to blow at Rosh Hashana. Crucifix.

Her Bible with the ivory cover. Our thick
comforters (good goose feather, not that chicken).
A donkey shoe, that's for good luck. My zither.
Little suit, the trousers buttoned onto the blouse.

My beaded wedding shoes. Certificates—these, all
vaccinations; this, meritorious service.
Three cupping glasses to draw out infections.
Picture locket (she was so small). Key to the house.

   Sit down. Look up. Keep your mouth shut.
   Not very long, the exposure.

        –ii–

Not much longer. We'll see the white cliffs, I promise.
Keep your life-jacket on. Hold my hand, don't cry.
Pray if you can. Make us to be warm again,
please God.
        The trudge over shingle, empty-handed.

Note:
Objects mentioned in the first three stanzas are on display, or described, at the Museum of Immigration, Ellis Island, New York, USA, along with beautiful identification photographs.

EVACUEES' OUTING, 1940

everybody in a bus to Sandy Bay
girls really annoying the way they have
of acting grown-up as if they knew things
but at least it'll be a chance to chuck pebbles

twelve o'clock and the tide's going out
and leaving a load of stuff behind   a dead bird
one foot and some feathers   head without eyes
girl says it's a razorbill cos she's got a book

it stinks   someone's picked up a mermaid's purse
that stinks too   the whole beach can get up your nose
like my grandma's bedroom   the sea has its own
tarry smell like Mr Carter who drives

sit down   the lady's handing out sandwiches
two grey slices with a pink bit   a hardboiled egg
treat   pick off the shell like it's my knees   oh great
being hungry once you get your teeth stuck in

plonk your feet on the ridges   think they're dry
but a rim of water bulges up   a desert
only wet with little holes   who pricked all them
and what made those curly shits when you're far out?

and anyway how can the sea tell the time
because the water's sliding up fast just at five
like they said only now it's changed   goosepimply
and grey   I can hear the lady shouting faintly

she's got the baskets stacked up and her blanket
and now she's waving at us   better hurry
my arm hurts with chucking so many stones
and I'm scratchy with sand   Mr Carter's stamped out

his fag end and climbed in and started to rev
he says they'll be putting scaffolding all along
so everything shut off for the Duration
and no more trips to the sea thank you very much

THE WOODEN HOUSE

That summer when we were sent away,
the sun used to roost every night
in the attic of the wooden house.
We could hear it cracking its bones.
It was a griffin, practising
a silent snarl. It was a serpent
sliding among the rafters, licking
at the heavy air we lay in.
It wouldn't let us pull the shadows
over our heads. It was a blade
still carrying the heat of the forge,
so flexible and thin it could slice
between our eyelids however tight
we shut them. We knew you must never
look at the sun because it would drill
a hole in your eye, but we couldn't
stop it spying, or stop our tears,
though we were bone dry at the root.
When in the end it slept, we felt
how cold we were under the damp sheet.

WHAT REMAINS

A thumb print in clay. One scrap
of a freckled shell, smudged
with an almost-colour.

Form that a hare made. She fled,
leaving a ghost of warmth. Teasings of fur
still trembled at the rim.

In the scoop of a pillow
when a head has been lifted,
a scent lingers, a thimbleful

of wavering air. Once I thought
I could warm your spirit like raindrops
in a cupped palm. What's preserved

in the hollow of this hand?
The seams it was born with.
A few blanched scars.

SKIN NARRATIVES

Body transcribes itself monkishly
over seven years, each edition
less well bound, the scribal errors
grosser, blanched code of scars
a faulty braille still legible
even in palimpsest
on the thin vellum of hands, shins, wrists,
record of accident and skirmish:

a tin I was trying to open
that opened me (the kitchen cupboard
leant and delivered a hard clout);
Aunt Jessie's favourite glass
shivered into arrows, sheaved there
in my bare foot; a neat
pearl-handled pocket-knife turned spiteful—
these stitch marks in my palm to prove it—

the bright, bulging cabochon of blood
amazed me. This zigzag? That's the streak
of white in my mother's brown hair.
She's on her knees, picking
gravel out of mine, and I bite
on the raw jolts of pain
in silence because Grandma's in mourning
for her scarlet begonias, smashed.

THESE HANDS

These hands have been dangling beside me
all along, links of padded bone,
though I've scarcely noticed: the first folds,
creases, indentations, written
into palms and digits well before
I barged two-fisted into air,
nervous finger-ends securely backed
with a slip of the same chitin
as rhinoceros horn, kestrel claw,
ladybird carapace, crab shell.

Masters of the dumbshow, guiding me
through seven ages, comforters,
thieves, warm as fleece, accusers, icy,
blind dancers in the rites of flesh,
sufferers, scratchers: now they are old
I blame them for stumbling about,
poor labourers, curling on their pain;
yet when I come to stretch my spine
in rough indifferent ground, they'll lie there
patiently beside me, like dogs.

CLINIC

Knees withstanding.
Feet sometimes at nod
with unshaped words.

Hands in couples,
each palm a parent
to the other.

Don't be anxious.
This is my body
bequeathed to me.

Each stillbound head
laden with its world,
solitary.

FALSE STEP

I love the ambivalent rhythm
of five, asymmetry of seven,
like a turmoil among rising birds
joining and breaking, the singleness
of a multitude. But my body,
now it's old, forfeits assurance, can't
any longer riff on what's delayed
or glide out of a syncopation
unscathed. Hankering after balance,
it hesitates, and the metre's tripped.
Lost, the security of the beat.
In a murmuration of starlings
the single bird that a peregrine
discerns, and separates, and beheads.

COUNTING

There's a reckoning desert tribesmen use:
One. One. Two is for twins. As for the rest,
More is the only measure. More of sand.
Of locusts. The More of cattle grazing
among acacias, shuffling to the close
before sunset, each to be counted home.

One, the brindled heifer. One, the grand bull,
the master, swinging a broken horn. One,
the spotted cow anxious for her full Two
of tawny calves, each noted, jostling in.
Firelight jumps. The heaving shadows settle.
A child cries. A leopard coughs. The stars pad by.

HOW THE STORY GOES

Stick in a pin at *Once* to stop things swinging
in the solar wind. Next comes *upon*,
to indicate the vantage point. Finally
a time—that's more problematical

but for now you may ignore it. Start to plait.
Almost everything arrives in threes
though not triplets because there's a lucky one
who, after tribulations, must win—

not that he's the cleverest of the brothers,
just that his pockets are full of hap.
The little dog follows him because he smells
of cheese. The bird in his hand wants crumbs.

He has an eye for unconsidered trifles,
this lad. Doesn't plan or calculate
but leaves it to the god of snakes and ladders
to come up with something: a princess,

for example. He has always had the knack
of improvisation.
                    So you feed
your story with any threes that come to hand
until suddenly it's long enough

like Rapunzel's hair. Up he shins, down they come
into sunshine. What will happen next
is hap again: living happily ever
after. And there you are, that's Time solved.

FIVE

The puzzle of five: how to resolve
the balance of three and two, two and three,
or the solitary dancer among couples.

In the system of Linnaeus, five stamens
may cohere or not. Is something proved?
Little children still sit cross-legged among daisies,

pulling petals in odds and evens.
At dusk, on the pistil of the blackbird's tongue,
five notes echo the ancient mode that shepherds knew.

Across the dusty lek of Olympia,
long before the wars of books, one pentateuch
of instruments, hands, feet, head, challenged another.

A basket of five small barley cobs,
gathered and shared again, crust by crust, has fed
five thousand, story after story, song by song.

Put out your hand like a beggar and show me
the delta of five. There are the finger-wires
of bats, the seal's dactyl stumps parcelled in leather

or the fusion of five into one,
racing surefooted over desert sand.
Tell me how five became, I'll give you five gold rings.

REFLEX

I loitered a whole afternoon in the turning of pages,
reading about sea anemones. *Random searches
conducted under maximum parsimony*

*could reveal instances of incongruence
between mitochondrial and nuclear markers.*
Nobody about.

The small waves breathed. The water
was cool and transparent, revealing
the colours of every pebble.

*The combined data were afterwards subjected
to a thousand rounds of bootstrap sampling
to assess support for clades.*

The red cliffs shone downwards in perfect calm.
Trees of minimum length were found at least five times
and my legs, shorter then, showed pink-pale,

distorted, hairs stuck with bubbles. There they hang,
the pale sea chrysanthemums.
I push my finger into an ivory mouth,

a single, weak siphonoglyph. Tentacles close
to swallow me. I pull back, wake into my book,
quivering like a shrimp.

THE ONE CHOSEN

Roiling out of the black, a net
as heavy as ocean, voids. The shoal
shatters to myriads in one thrash.

Life on life goes flackering down deck,
snatching at air with bloody gills,
to be gutted and boxed, iced and priced.

They look lovely, fanned on the slab,
patterns of the sea still on their backs.
Fillet him for you?
                              No, like that.

At the evening ritual, I admire
my choice again. His silent mouth
opens formally in the pan.

THE GARDENER

Once I found a glove, and bent to pick it up—
nothing but leaves. I glimpsed him then. The dull
shine on a khaki waistcoat. Rubbing his jaw—
the little rasp was the whisper of dry grass.

A thinking man, taking his time, hands patient
as plough horses in the furrow, pondering
the small green rows. Yet he seemed not to see
the dandelions shining beside his boot

or bindweed loitering through. Ground elder
had obliterated the path. Perhaps
he was blind, I thought. Did he know I was there?
My presence accidental, a cloud passing.

How long the trace of him lasted, I can't tell.
After a while, he faded. The robin,
who had known his ways, watched me, and was soon gone,
needing his patch as it had been, his habits,

the ancient patterns. I wasn't real to him—
forgotten, or not formed. Time was contracting
into a single sphere, encompassing
all that was ever made. The infant birches

I had pushed through were grown and fallen. Mare's tail,
the green brush I trod, hardened into forest.
My echo swung in a gulf of echoes
long before garden or gardener were made.

WHAT THE BIRD SAID

Flick of shadow, chip of song.
A robin came, glancing,
turned the puff of himself
towards me, rosehip or copperleaf
according to light;
opened his beak on a winter breath,
shook out tremors of music.

A loss, a death, was stuck
hard as a gall in my throat.
I was foolish for consolation,
wanting a god to be angry with.
Shadows. December sun.
Oak apples, twigs, dry leaves. A bird.
Nothing but this, it said.

MOTE

That black crumb of flotsam, which doesn't
float but slips at capricious angles
across walls and windows, or the glaze
of a passing cloud, butts in on me
like the false note a child keeps hitting
in some dull, familiar practice piece
(*F sharp, can't you*) and now executes
diagonals on my page. I'm vexed,
try slaughtering it with blinks. No good.
Feign patience and try to seduce it
into focus for a gorgon stare
but it doodles an insect flourish,
skips into some blind anchorage, waits
till it's forgotten, and sidles back.

THE END

I am odl an don seee towell
i can no longre TYPe   Whic
his a nisence. Pety I'm a Pot.
 i dont wan'to post so what can I
dobut in vent a styl of my one,
rewit all pems agangule,
 in some rar nugalage, and galaunge
the hole thing off course in Sybillics.

DUNNERHOLM

Still at an ebb, the tide. We crossed
the cockleshell wastes, and started
over quilted surfaces of mud and sand.
Under the pressure of every step
rose gleaming rims of water.
Our tracks unravelled crookedly
like rope eased overboard.

Lifting at times from draining sands
a fan of wings shook open, white
or silver against the opposite headland's
green and ochre margins. Far Black Combe
stood shadowy, a sheer hulk.
The hills were fledged with snow. The sea
glinted with armoured mills.

But she had known that shore as I
had not. Warnings and childhood fears
spoke in her like the lisp of a tide sliding
in quickening panes, and so we turned
towards Dunnerholm, our place
of safety, where we would shelter
and talk and take the sun.

As I think of it now, the light
has ebbed away, leaving a hunched
and darkening hause of rock hooded in gorse
and scrubby elder. There's not a sound
but the pitchless lick and lap
of a tide filling. Dunnerholm.
I shan't go there again.

PEBBLE

The tide has swept it glistening here
for me to glean. At once I love
the blueness of its weight, the slip
of iridescence in a skin of quartz.

But now it's in my palm, orphaned
from water, it takes on dullness
as though a vein had clogged, the way
a dying animal loses lustre,

so I give it back to the sea,
and go on hunting for the stone
I shall never find, which will hold,
till seas run dry, its mastery of light.

ABOUT THE AUTHOR

Meg Peacocke grew up in South Devon in a musical family. Her brother was the composer Richard Rodney Bennett (1936–2012); she collaborated with him on a number of vocal and choral works from the 1980s onwards.

She read English at Oxford, but spent more time on *a capella* singing and playing the oboe than on literary studies. After years of teaching, travel, marriage, bringing up four children, training in counselling and working in the children's cancer unit of Addenbrooke's Hospital, she moved to a small hill farm in Cumbria where she lived for twenty-five years, running the smallholding single-handed.

Although she had written poems since childhood, it was only in her fifties that she began seriously publishing: first, four collections from Peterloo Poets, then two from Shoestring Press, followed by an illustrated prose memoir. Together with artist Pip Hall, she was involved in the Poetry Path, a series of twelve poems based on a year in the life of a hill farmer. These were carved onto stone blocks and placed along a walking route either side of the River Eden, near Kirkby Stephen.

Her hill-farming days now behind her, she currently lives in County Durham, where she continues to write.

⚜